Newcastle Libraries and Information Service

☎ **0845 002 0336**

Due for return	Due for return	Due for return

Please return this item to any of Newcastle's Libraries by the last
date shown above. ff not requested by another customer the loan
can be renewed, you can do this by phone, post or in person.
Charges may be made for late returns.

www.heinemann.co.uk/library
Visit our website to find out more information about Heinemann L

To order:
☎ Phone 44 (0) 1865 888066
▤ Send a fax to 44 (0) 1865 314091
▣ Visit the Heinemann Bookshop at www.heinemann.co.uk/library to
catalogue and order online.

First published in Great Britain by Heinemann Library,
Halley Court, Jordan Hill, Oxford OX2 8EJ, part of Pearson
Education. Heinemann is a registered trademark of Pearson
Education Ltd.

© Pearson Education Ltd 2008
First published in paperback in 2009
The moral right of the proprietor has been asserted.

Editorial: Charlotte Guillain and Vicki Yates
Design: Victoria Bevan, Joanna Hinton-Malivoire
and Q2A solutions
Picture research: Ruth Blair and Q2A solutions
Production: Duncan Gilbert

Printed and bound in China by South China
Printing Co. Ltd.

ISBN 978 0 431 191843 (Hardback)

ISBN 978 0431 19192 8 (Paperback)
13 12 11 10 09
10 9 8 7 6 5 4 3 2 1

British Library C
Yates, Vicki
Travel. - (Then and now)
1. Travel - Juvenile literature 2. Travel - History - Juvenile
literature
910
A full catalogue record for this book is available from the
British Library.

Acknowledgements
The publishers would like to thank the following for permission
to reproduce photographs:
Alamy pp. **4** (Frances Roberts/Alamy), **22** (Bill Boston);
Airbus pp. **5**, **17**; AP Images p. **18**; Courtesy of The
Bancroft Library p. **20** (University of California, Berkeley);
Bionik Media p. **6**; Daimler Chrysler p. **9**; Ford Media pp.
5, **11**; Honda p. **23**; NASA pp. **19**, **23**; Phil Derner, Jr p. **7**
(Airliners.net); Photolibrary.com pp. **13** (David Messent),
14 (Index Stock Imagery), **15** (Photo Researchers, Inc),
16 (Science Photo Library), **21** (Index Stock Imagery);
Puget Sound Maritime Historical Society pp. **12**, **23**; San
Francisco Public Library p. **8**; Science & Society Picture
Library p. **10** (Science Museum Archive); Shutterstock p. **5**

Cover photograph of plane reproduced with permission
of Alamy (BL Images Ltd) and photograph of horse and
cart reproduced with permission of Getty Images (Robert
Harding). Back cover photograph of steam train reproduced
with permission of Photolibrary.com (Index Stock Imagery).

Every effort has been made to contact copyright holders
of any material reproduced in this book. Any omissions
will be rectified in subsequent printings if notice is given
to the publishers.

Contents

What is travel?

Travelling is moving from place to place.

People can travel in many ways.

Long ago it took a long time
to travel.

Today it takes a short time
to travel.

Long ago animals helped people move around.

Today we use vehicles with **engines** to help us move around.

Travel by road

Long ago cars were cold
and uncomfortable.

Today cars are warm and comfortable.

Travel on water

Long ago boats used sails to move.

Today boats can use engines
to move.

Travel by rail

Long ago trains moved slowly.

Today trains can move very fast.

Travel in the sky

pilot

Long ago aeroplanes were
very small.

Today aeroplanes are very big.

Long ago it was hard to travel far.

Today we can even travel
into space.

Let's compare

Long ago travel was very different.

Which is better? Then or now?

What is it?

tool

Long ago this tool was used for travel.
Do you know what it is?

Answer on p. 24

Picture glossary

engine machine that makes things work

sail piece of cloth attached on a boat

space area outside Earth where the stars and planets are

Index

Answer to question on p. 22 This is a starting handle. People used it to start the engine in cars and other vehicles.

Note to Parents and Teachers

Before reading

Ask the children how they got to school. How do they travel when they are going on holiday or to see someone a long way away? Have they ever been on a train or a plane? Did it go fast or slow?

After reading

• Using catalogues or magazines, ask the children to cut out pictures of the different vehicles. Make a collage of all the different ways people travel today. Ask the children if they can tell you how things have changed. Write captions under the different vehicles saying how these have changed over time e.g. "Cars were slow and noisy."

• Tell the children to move around as if they were riding an old heavy bicycle and then ask them to change and pedal as fast as they can on a new bike. Repeat with cars, trains, ships and planes.

•Teach: "Twinkle, twinkle chocolate bar/My dad drives a rusty car/Push the lever, pull the choke/Off we go in a cloud of smoke./Twinkle, twinkle chocolate bar/My dad drives a rusty car."